BOY WITH A MISSION

BOY WITH A MISSION

The Life of Francis Marto of Fatima

WRITTEN AND ILLUSTRATED
BY THE
DAUGHTERS OF ST. PAUL

ST. PAUL EDITIONS

NIHIL OBSTAT:
  Rev. Shawn G. Sheehan
  Diocesan Censor

IMPRIMATUR:
  + Richard Cardinal Cushing

ISBN 0-8198-0229-8

Library of Congress Catalog Card Number: 65-24081

Copyright © 1981, 1967 by the Daughters of St. Paul

Printed in the U.S.A. by the Daughters of St. Paul
50 St. Paul's Ave., Boston, MA 02130

The Daughters of St. Paul are an international congregation of religious women serving the Church with the communications media.

CONTENTS

Part I

"I Don't Mind" 13

"Do Not Be Afraid" 19

"He, Too, Will Come...." 25

"Pray Like This...." 31

"I'm Not Coming!" 37

"Sacrifice Yourselves...." 42

"I Want To Console" 46

Part II

"You Two Drink First" 53

"We Would Rather Die!" 58

"We'll Fry Them Like Fish!" 63

"The Lord Is Pleased...." 68

"Look at the Sun!" 71

"I Can't Bless" 75

"What a Beautiful Light!" 81

PART I

*When I behold Your heavens,
the work of Your fingers,
the moon and the stars which
You set in place–
What is man that You
should be mindful of him,
or the son of man that
You should care for him?*

PSALMS

CHAPTER 1

"I DON'T MIND"

They were poor boys, who lived in a small town among the lonely mountains of Portugal. Almost any bright object was a novelty, and certainly Francis Marto's handkerchief had to be seen and admired by all.

Someone had brought eight-year-old Francis the handkerchief from a famous Marian shrine, and it had a brightly-colored picture of the Madonna painted on it. "Let's see," exclaimed his companions eagerly and the handkerchief was passed from hand to hand.

"I wish I had one like that!"

"So do I!"

Suddenly the handkerchief disappeared into one boy's pocket.

"Hey, thief! That belongs to Francis!" And another boy tried to grab the handkerchief away. A fight was starting, but Francis Marto stopped it at once. "Let him keep it," he said. "I don't mind."

Francis was always like that. He would give up just about anything as long as he made someone happy. He did not know it that day, but soon he would be giving up things for God, too, just as he was now giving up his new handkerchief for a companion.

✳

Francis' town of Fatima is a tiny mountain village in the center of Portugal. Its people are poor and simple. The men work in the fields; the women take care of the homes and sew and weave cloth. The children tend their parents' sheep in the pastures on the slopes of the rocky mountains. They carry their lunches with them and stay in the fields from morning to evening, returning home at night to join their parents for supper and the family rosary.

This was the simple daily routine of the famous "Children of Fatima"–Francis, Lucy and Jacinta–before the marvelous events which changed their lives in 1917.

Francis Marto was born on June 11, 1908, the tenth child in the Marto family. His sister Jacinta was born two years later. Their cousin, Lucy Dos Santos, was a year older than Francis. These three became close friends.

When they were old enough to tend their families' sheep, Lucy, Francis and Jacinta would wake up early every morning, and before the sun dispersed the mists from the valleys, they would be off for the pasture with their flocks. What did it matter to leave their

"I DON'T MIND" 15

beds and interrupt their dreams when soon they would be enjoying themselves in the wide open spaces?

Lucy knew every nook and corner of the territory, and could always find the best pasture land–peaceful mountain slopes covered with brightly colored flowers.

As they hurried their flocks on towards the pasture, the bleating of the sheep mingled with the children's prayers—the Our Father, the Hail Mary, the Angel of God.... Later on, after lunch, they would recite the rosary together.

The rosary was a family tradition, and traditions have to be respected. Of course, the rosary can seem a very long prayer to three children who are anxious to play! So one of them–probably the lively Jacinta–suggested a way out. Instead of saying the complete prayers, one of the trio would say, "Hail Mary," and the others would answer simply, "Holy Mary." At the end of each decade they would all say, "Our Father." In this way the rosary was "said" in the space of a minute! Then they would return to their games. Often Francis would play his reed flute while Lucy and Jacinta would dance.

❋

The three cousins had very different characters.

Lucy was the leader of the little group. She was lively and cheerful.

Jacinta, too, was quick and lively, but she was much more sensitive and vain than Lucy. She liked to have her own way, and if someone said something that offended her she would cry at once.

Francis was slower and more thoughtful. Although he had good ideas, he usually let Lucy take the lead. He was deeply conscious of the feelings of others and usually let them have their own way–except when it was a matter of right and wrong.

Francis enjoyed playing with the other village boys, but he did not mind at all when he lost. Some of the other boys would take advantage of his good nature, and demand that the game be played over if Francis had happened to win it. He would give in at once, saying, "All right; it doesn't matter to me."

But there were other times when he would leave a game right in the middle. If one of the other boys asked, "Why are you going?" he would say, "Because you're bad," or simply, "Because I want to." He meant that they were doing or saying something wrong.

"I DON'T MIND" 17

In most things he was a typical outdoor boy. He liked animals and used to roll snakes and lizards around with a stick and make them drink sheep's milk which he poured into a hollow of rock. Often he brought these pets home, where they were anything but popular with his mother! How many times did she have to exclaim, "Francis, please take that snake out of here!" Another of his favorite pastimes was practical joking, with his older brother John the prime target. Whenever John went to sleep, he had no way of knowing what he would find in his open mouth when he woke up.

But, although mischievous, Francis was kind, both to people and to animals. One day he met a boy who had caught a little bird. "Don't keep him like that," said Francis. "Can't you see how unhappy he is? Let him go!"

But the other boy sensed a way to make some money. "I won't let him go," he said. "You buy him from me." And Francis did–with a little bit of money that was all he had.

In the countryside, Francis hunted out the dens of rabbits, foxes and porcupines among the bushes, waded in the clear mountain brooks and sat under chestnut trees, playing his homemade reed flute and mimicking bird calls.

He was especially fond of the sun, which he called the "lamp of God." How beautiful it was when it rose in the morning, scattering its reflection over the dewdrops to transform them into diamonds, or when it set in the evening and its splendor blazed from the window panes of houses and barns up and down the mountain slopes. What great bursts of light it sent out just before darkness came to swallow up the earth! "No lamp is as beautiful as the Lord's!" he would exclaim to Lucy and Jacinta.

Soon he was to see sights far more wonderful.

Chapter 2

"DO NOT BE AFRAID"

In the spring of 1916 World War I was raging, and claiming victims on all its fronts. Many good Portuguese families were in mourning for their loved ones.

One day Francis, Lucy and Jacinta had eaten their lunch in a mountainside shelter, and, after quickly "saying" the rosary, had started to play a game. Suddenly a strong gust of wind made them raise their heads. Above the olive orchard at the foot of the hill, they saw a white figure standing in mid air.

Was it the "man in the white sheet" whom Lucy and some other companions had seen in the distance the year before? Yes, it was, but this time the strange figure was coming toward them. The form was transparent and sparkled like crystal. Joy, wonder, and fear welled up in their hearts.

As soon as it had come near them, the figure smiled and said, "Do not be afraid. I am the angel of peace. Pray with me." They obeyed. They knelt, bowed down until their foreheads touched the ground, and repeated everything the angel said.

"My God, I believe, I adore, I hope, I love You. I ask Your pardon for all who do not believe, do not adore, do not hope, and do not love You."

After repeating this three times, the angel stood up. "Pray thus," he said. "The Hearts of Jesus and Mary are prepared to listen to your prayers."

Then he disappeared.

Faint and absorbed, they repeated the same prayer, as though forced to do so by an unknown power. They told no one of this experience.

✻

Months passed. Summer came. One day the three shepherds were playing beside the well in Lucy's yard.

Suddenly the same figure appeared beside them.

"What are you doing?" he asked. "Pray, pray much. The Hearts of Jesus and Mary have wonderful plans for you....

Offer prayers and sacrifices to the Most High."

"Sacrifices? How?" Lucy dared to ask.

"In all that you can, offer a sacrifice as an act of reparation for the many sins with which God is offended and as a supplication for the conversion of sinners. In this way you will bring peace to your country. I am the Guardian Angel of Portugal. Above all, accept and bear with patience the sufferings which the Lord will send you."

Prostrated with their foreheads upon the ground the children prayed for some time. When they recovered, Francis asked, "Lucy, you spoke with an angel. What did he tell you?"

"What?" exclaimed Lucy, "Didn't you hear what he said?"

"No. I saw that he spoke with you. I heard what you said, but not one word of what the angel said," answered Francis.

But the experience had been too overpowering for Lucy to tell it yet. "Listen, Francis, ask me tomorrow. That is...ask Jacinta, if you wish."

"Jacinta!" exclaimed Francis. "You tell me what the angel said."

But even Jacinta answered as Lucy had, "Tomorrow!"

❀

Francis waited. But it was a long night of short naps, interrupted by moments of anxiety and an excited waiting for the break of dawn, which finally came.

"Did you sleep last night?" he asked Lucy as soon as he met her.

"Of course! Didn't you?"

"No. I kept thinking of the angel and of what he said to you."

Then Lucy told him, with Francis interrupting to ask questions. "Who is the Most High? Why is the Lord offended? And why does He suffer so much?"

The answer to this last question impressed the boy more than all the others. How it hurt him to see anyone suffer! And to think of Jesus suffering because of the sins of men. . . .

"If Jesus suffers, it is necessary to console Him," he thought. He thought about this for a while, then he asked more questions. This caused Jacinta to fear.

"Be careful not to tell anyone about this! In these things speak very little."

Francis understood. Later Jacinta confided that she could not speak or play and did not have the strength to do anything, after seeing the angel. Francis agreed with her.

He said, "Neither can I. But what does it matter? The angel is better than anything. Let's think of him."

✱

Two or three months had gone by when the angel appeared a third time. He held a chalice in his hand. Above the chalice there was a white Host from which drops of Blood were falling.

Chalice and Host miraculously remained in mid air while the angel prostrated himself and repeated three times:

"Most Holy Trinity, Father, Son and Holy Spirit, I adore You profoundly, and I offer You the Most Precious Body, Blood, soul and divinity of Our Lord Jesus Christ present in all the tabernacles of the world, in reparation for the outrages with which He Himself is offended. Through the infinite merits of His Most Sacred Heart and the intercession of the Immaculate Heart of Mary, I ask of You the conversion of poor sinners."

He arose. Taking the miraculous Host, he gave It to Lucy who consumed It. Then he gave the chalice to Jacinta and to Francis. They drank.

"Take," said the angel, "the Body and Blood of Jesus horribly insulted by ungrateful men. Make reparation for their crimes. Console your God."

The angel prostrated himself again, repeated the prayer three times and disappeared forever, leaving the children in ecstasy, absorbed in prayer.

Later Francis, who had not heard the angel's words, asked, "Lucy, I know the angel gave you Holy Communion, but how about Jacinta and me?"

"That was Communion, too, Francis. Didn't you see the Blood that dripped down into the chalice from the Host?"

Francis was satisfied. "I knew that God was in me," he said, "but I didn't know exactly how." Then he knelt in love and thanksgiving to repeat and repeat the beautiful prayer.

"I like to see the angel very much," he said later on, "but the worst of it is that afterwards we are unable to do anything. I can't even walk. I don't know what's wrong with me."

CHAPTER 3

"HE, TOO, WILL COME...."

On Sunday, May 13, 1917, the cousins assisted at Mass in the parish church and then decided to take the sheep to Cova da Iria.

The Cova is a valley about two miles from Fatima. There Lucy's parents owned a small lot upon which a few holm-oaks and olive trees grew.

While the flocks went about feeding upon the best grass, the three friends played games and told stories. Lucy, who was ten years old, was a good story teller. She could not read, never having gone to school, but she had a very good memory. Whenever her mother read stories from the Gospels and the Old Testament, Lucy listened attentively, remembering them faithfully and repeated the stories accurately. Francis and Jacinta liked to listen to them.

After lunch, they knelt down to recite the rosary as usual. The fresh spring grass, the shelter of a cave, and the shade of a chestnut tree wonderfully inspired them, as the beads passed through their fingers. After the rosary, they returned to their games.

The sun shone clearly in the sky, and many field flowers bowed their heads before its hot rays. Suddenly there was an unexpected flash of lightning. The three children looked at each other in wonder.

"Do you think that a storm is coming up from behind the mountain?" asked Lucy.

Although the horizon was clear, with no clouds in sight, it was better to play safe.

"Shall we go home?" they asked each other.

"Yes, let's go."

In a moment the flock was rounded up and urged down the hillside. Another flash of lightning cut across their path. This time they were really frightened. They started to run, hoping to arrive home before the storm broke. But when they reached the bottom of the valley, they stopped, as though by command.

❂

A few steps away from them, upon a small green holm-oak tree, a beautiful Lady looked down at them and invited them to come near to her.

The three children were afraid and wanted to run away, but she reassured them, "Do not be afraid. I do not wish to harm you."

Francis, being sensitive by nature, was touched at once by her sadness.

Jacinta and Francis looked up at her in wonder, while Lucy tried to find the correct words with which to address the Lady.

The Lady appeared to be about sixteen years old. Her white dress, drawn tight at the neck by a golden cord, fell to her feet. A white mantle bordered with gold covered her head and almost her entire person. In her hands, she held a white rosary with a silver cross. The whole vision shown like crystal in the sun.

The Lady was not standing in mid-air, but rested lightly upon the little holm-oak tree, just barely touching its leaves. Her face, of heavenly beauty, was veiled with sadness.

Francis, being sensitive by nature, was touched at once by her sadness.

"Where are you from?" Lucy asked.

"My country is heaven."

The Lady was so sweet in answering that Lucy was encouraged to continue.

"What do you desire?"

"I have come to ask you to come here at the same hour on the 13th every month, for six months in a row, until October. Then I will tell you who I am and what I wish."

Lucy found it easy to speak to the Lady, whose presence was not overpowering like that of the angel. Confidently she asked:

"HE, TOO, WILL COME...."

"If you come from heaven, tell me, will I go there?"

"Yes."

"And Jacinta?"

"Jacinta, too."

"And Francis?"

The eyes of the Lady rested upon the nine-year-old boy, with a thoughtful, motherly gaze. Was there a tinge of disapproval in her expression?

"He too will come; but first he will have to say many rosaries."

Encouraged by the Lady's goodness, Lucy asked about two little girls who had died recently. The Lady replied that one was in heaven, the other in purgatory. Then she continued, "Will you offer yourselves to God, ready to make sacrifices and willingly to accept all the sufferings He will send you, in order to make reparation for the sins with which the Divine Majesty is offended, to obtain the conversion of sinners?"

Lucy answered for the three of them, "Yes, we want to."

The Lady showed her approval with a lovely smile. Then she added, "You will have to suffer much, but the grace of God will assist and comfort you always."

Then, opening her hands, which had been

joined, she let a ray of mysterious light fall upon them. The light seemed to cut right into their hearts and souls. Somehow they knew that the light was God; in fact, they felt embraced by God. Lucy, Jacinta and Francis fell to their knees, and repeated acts of adoration and of love.

The Lady had one more recommendation: "Say the rosary every day, to obtain peace for the world." Then suddenly she rose from the treetop and moved off toward the east until a blaze of light enveloped her and she disappeared.

While the vision of the angel had made the children unable to speak—often for a few hours—the vision of the Lady had filled them with such peace and joy that they began to talk at once. Francis, again, had not heard the vision's words, but Lucy immediately told him all. When he heard that he would go to heaven after he had said many rosaries, he jumped for joy and exclaimed, "Oh, my Lady, my Lady! I will say as many rosaries as you wish!"

And he would keep his promise.

CHAPTER 4

"PRAY LIKE THIS...."

After the vision had passed, they did not feel like playing. The girls talked about the Lady all afternoon while Francis listened silently, lost in thought. Many rosaries? Of course, he would say many, if this was what God and the beautiful Lady wanted him to do.

Perhaps he remembered the couple of times he had refused to say his night prayers — until his father had straightened him out! There would be no more refusals to pray from Francis, now that he had caught a glimpse of the wonder and splendor of God and the sweet sadness of the Lady.

✷

Lucy, who had been teased so much about "the man in the sheet," decided that it was best for them not to talk about what had happened. No one would believe them for sure.

At dusk, they started home. Jacinta's heart was overflowing, and she broke the silence now and then by jumping with joy and exclaiming, "What a beautiful Lady!"

"I bet you'll tell someone about her right away," warned Lucy.

"Oh, no," Jacinta promised. "We won't say a word, will we Francis?"

"No," promised her brother. "We won't."

✿

Like a small river which swells and swells and then overflows its banks, Jacinta soon felt as if she would burst. That secret just *had* to come out! And so, Jacinta told her mother as soon as she saw her.

Francis looked at his little sister in amazement, and no doubt he felt like giving her a little kick to make her keep quiet, but it was too late. Now, what could he do? He had to speak, now that the secret was out, but rather than give anything else away, he simply agreed to all that Jacinta had said.

Mrs. Marto did not believe the story, and told Lucy's mother, who became very upset. She thought that the three children were telling lies. It is a dreadful thing not to be believed! The sufferings of Lucy, Francis and Jacinta were beginning.

"PRAY LIKE THIS...."

June 13 finally came.

At the appointed hour, the three young shepherds were kneeling at the Cova da Iria, saying the rosary. Ever since the Lady had appeared to them, they had said the Our Fathers and Hail Marys of the rosary completely.

A few people had come, out of curiosity, and were whispering among themselves nearby.

Suddenly the children saw the lightning, and ran toward the three-foot holm-oak above which the Lady had appeared the first time. The Lady appeared, smiling as before.

"What do you wish?" Lucy asked.

"I wish you to come here on the 13th of next month, and to recite the rosary every day. After each one of the mysteries, my children, I want you to pray like this: *O my Jesus, forgive us and deliver us from the fire of hell. Take all souls to heaven, especially those who are most in need.* I also want you to learn how to read and write. Later I will tell you what else I desire."

Lucy asked for the cure of a sick person.

"Tell him to lead a better life and he will get well within the year," answered the Lady. Then she confided a secret to them, telling them not to reveal it to anyone.

What could it be? Many people tried to guess. But only in 1927 was it known for sure, when Lucy was told by Jesus Himself to reveal part of it. Lucy had said, "I would like to ask you to bring all three of us to heaven."

"Yes," answered the Lady, "I will come for Francis and Jacinta very soon! You, however, must remain here on earth a longer time. Jesus wants to use you to make my Immaculate Heart better known and loved."

"Then I shall remain alone?" Lucy asked sadly.

"No, my daughter. I will never abandon you. My Immaculate Heart will be your refuge and the way which will lead you to God."

In pronouncing these last words, the Blessed Virgin—for it must be she!—opened her hands and let the great light shine upon them again. They saw themselves in the light as if they were submerged in God. Jacinta and Francis seemed to be in the part of the light that represented heaven, and Lucy in the part that shone on the earth. A heart encircled with piercing thorns could suddenly be seen in the Lady's hand.

✽

People can be mean, and some of those who followed the three shepherds back to the village, were just that. They teased and taunted:

"Lucy, did the Lady dance on the top of the tree?"

"Jacinta, why are you so quiet? Cat got your tongue?"

"Are you a saint yet, Jacinta?"

The lack of reverence toward the Lady was especially hard to bear.

Only when they were together by themselves could they talk about what they had seen. Then, Francis asked, "Why does Our Lady stand with a heart in her hand, and shine that great light of God on the world? Lucy, you were standing in the light which shone down upon the earth; Jacinta and I were in the light which shone heavenward."

"Because," explained Lucy, "Jacinta and you will go to heaven soon, while I will remain on earth for a while."

"How many years, do you think?"

"I don't know, but I believe many."

"Did the Virgin tell you?"

"No. I saw it in the light which she was putting into our chest."

"It is just so," approved Jacinta, who had been following the conversation attentively. "I saw the same thing."

"What did the Lady tell you?"

"What is the secret?"

The women of Fatima were dying of feminine curiosity, and the more the children refused to disclose their secret, the more curious the questioners became. One day some women, dressed in their Sunday best and sporting gold jewelry, came to visit the Marto family. One of them showed her bracelets and necklace to Jacinta. "Do you like these?" she asked.

"Yes," replied Jacinta honestly.

"Would you like to have them?"

"Of course," said Jacinta. She was only seven, and did not sense the snare which was being laid for her.

"Then tell us your secret!" exclaimed the woman, and she took off the jewelry and held it out toward Jacinta.

The little girl was horrified. "Don't!" she exclaimed. "Please don't! I can't tell you anything! I couldn't tell you the secret if you gave me the whole world!"

CHAPTER 5

"I'M NOT COMING!"

Towards the end of June, the pastor sent for Mrs. Dos Santos, saying that he wished to see her together with Lucy.

"Finally!" sighed Mrs. Dos Santos, in relief. "Father will drive these crazy ideas out of Lucy's head!"

"Listen," she warned Lucy, "tomorrow we are going to assist at Mass; then you will go to see the pastor. Let him punish you. Let him do whatever he wishes. I will be happy, as long as he obliges you to confess that you have lied."

Lucy kept silent; but as soon as she had the chance, she warned Francis and Jacinta.

"We are going, too," said her cousins. "The pastor has asked our mother to take us to him. But she did not say that he would hurt us."

The next day, they were questioned by the pastor, very carefully, but without any threats. He tried to make them contradict each other—but can the truth ever contradict itself?

Of course, there were some things that they had been forbidden to say at all. This caused the pastor to tell Lucy's mother, "It doesn't seem to me that this comes from heaven. When the Lord reveals Himself to souls, He generally commands them to tell everything to their confessors or pastors. Lucy, instead, closes herself up in silence. It can be a trick of the devil. The future will reveal the truth."

A trick of the devil? How this expression disturbed Lucy! It bothered her so much that she even had a nightmare about it and began to ask herself if it would not be better to say that she had not seen the vision after all. This would end the matter, and peace would be restored at home.

But when she mentioned it to her cousins, Francis was horrified. "Do not do it, for goodness sake! You would be telling a lie, and a lie is a sin."

"All right," said Lucy at once, "I won't. But I'm not going to the Cova any more."

"What?" exclaimed Francis. "Didn't the Lady say that we would have to suffer much in order to make reparation? And you are so sad, while with this suffering we could make reparation? Let's be happy!"

"I'm not going to the Cova any more."

Lucy understood all this. She wanted to see the beautiful Lady, but she did not feel that she could bear more punishment and insults. She began to avoid the company of her cousins. She would hide when they looked for her and say nothing when they called her name.

The night of July 12, the little town was in a commotion. In the streets, at the corners, and in the houses everyone was talking about the apparitions. An echo of all this reached Lucy. She desired to see the heavenly Lady again—but what if all this were the work of the devil?

Lucy went to her cousins' house. In the old courtyard, in the light of the moon, Francis came happily to meet her.

"Then you're coming with us tomorrow?" he asked joyfully.

"No, I'm not coming. I've told you already that I'm never coming to the Cova again."

"Oh, what a shame!" exclaimed Francis. "Why do you think such things now? Can't you see that it can't be the devil? God is already so sorrowful because of the sins which are committed, and if you do not come to the Cova now, He will be even more sad. Please come."

"No. You're wasting your breath."

What a disappointment for Jacinta! What a disappointment for Francis who feared to displease the Lord, Whom he wanted to console.

"Believe me," he later confided to Lucy, "that night I didn't sleep a wink, and I spent the night weeping and praying to the Blessed Mother to make you come."

And what was that irresistable force that, unexpectedly urged Lucy to go to her cousins' house on the morning of the 13th? Was it the Virgin, who had heard the prayers of Francis and Jacinta? We do not know, but the fact is that Lucy found Jacinta and Francis kneeling in their room weeping and praying.

"How come you're still here?" she asked. "Why didn't you go? It's late!"

"We didn't dare go without you."

"I'm on my way," Lucy replied.

The three cousins went to the Cova. A large crowd had gathered there, and they had difficulty in making their way to the holm-oak tree.

Chapter 6

"SACRIFICE YOURSELVES...."

On that hot, muggy July day it was difficult to breathe beneath the sun's burning rays.

The eyes of the crowd were attentively fixed upon the three children. At the sound of the noonday bells, the Lady returned, surrounded by a halo of light, but Lucy did not have the courage to speak to her.

Jacinta encouraged her, "Come, Lucy, speak! Don't you see that she is already here and wishes to speak to you?"

Overcoming her fear, Lucy asked, "What do you wish?"

The Lady repeated the same requests she had made before, and at Lucy's begging, she added that she would reveal her name in October, and that she would work a miracle then, also. She added, "Sacrifice yourselves for sinners and say often, but especially when making a sacrifice, *O Jesus, it is for Your love, for the conversion of sinners and in reparation for the offenses to the Immaculate Heart of Mary.*"

But the conversation was not ended. At a certain point, the three children grew pale, and trembled. Lucy screamed. The crowd, which could see nothing but the children's expressions, shuddered with fear.

At the end of the vision, the children remained deep in their thoughts. The spectators, who had seen a white cloud, which dimmed the brightness of the sun as it descended upon the holm-oak, understood that the apparition was over. The sun became bright. The people crowded around the three children and showered them with questions.

Lucy made every effort to answer them as best as she could.

"Why were you so sad?" they asked. "Why did you scream and tremble?"

It was a secret. The Blessed Virgin had forbidden them to tell. They remained faithful to her command.

The secret is known now in part, because Lucy was later permitted to reveal it.

The Virgin had shown the children a terrifying vision of hell—an ocean of fire. Buried in the flames were ugly, horrible demons, similar to unknown and terrifying beasts, transparent as glowing coals of fire—human forms, black and discolored, rising above the flames only to fall down into their midst again, with screams of pain and desperation which made the children tremble with fear. Hell!

The three children had looked toward the Virgin in order to overcome their terror. The Lady had talked to them lovingly and sadly.

"You have seen hell, where the souls of poor unrepentant sinners go. To save them, God wants to establish devotion to my Immaculate Heart. If what I tell you will be done, many souls will be saved and there will be peace. But if it will not be done, if God does not cease to be offended, Divine Justice will make itself manifest with new and more serious punishments.

"An irreverent propaganda will sow many errors in the world, instigating wars and persecutions against the Church. Many good people will be martyred and the Holy Father will have much to suffer. Many nations will be destroyed.

"The present war is about to end. But if people do not cease to offend God, not many years will pass by before another and worse war will break out. When you will see the night illumined by an unknown light, that will be the sign God will give you—that the world is about to be punished through war, famine, and persecutions against the Church and the Holy

"SACRIFICE YOURSELVES...."

Father. I will come to ask that the world be consecrated to my Immaculate Heart, and that Communion be received in reparation on the first Saturday of every month. If my wishes are fulfilled ... there will be peace; otherwise. ... Remember, do not tell this to anyone except Francis."

As usual, Francis had seen, but had not heard.

Chapter 7

"I WANT TO CONSOLE"

The same ray of sunlight often has different effects. Passing through an odd-shaped piece of glass, it breaks up into a thousand bright colors. Falling directly on a white wall, it makes that wall as blinding as snow; when passing through a hand or a leaf, it makes the object seem to glow from within.

Just so, Francis, Jacinta and Lucy responded differently to the same apparitions. Lucy was to spread devotion to the Immaculate Heart of Mary, Jacinta was to make reparation for sinners. And Francis? He, too, was finding his vocation–his mission in life.

"I liked the angel very much," Francis said to Lucy and Jacinta, "and I enjoyed seeing the Blessed Virgin even more. But what impressed me the most was seeing God in that great light." He had felt so powerfully attracted to God that his thoughts turned to Him naturally from then on. The boy who had once refused to say his night prayers would henceforward find prayer as natural as breathing.

"I like God very much," Francis continued, "but He—Jesus—is so sad because of so many sins! In order to comfort Jesus, we must never sin."

One day Lucy asked him, "Francis, which do you like the most: to console God or to convert sinners so that they will not go to hell?"

At once Francis answered, "I want to console God. Just last month, didn't you notice how the Virgin became sad when she said that mankind should not offend God, Who is already so much offended? I want to console God first, and then convert mankind so that they won't offend Him any more."

During those summer months while the sheep browsed in the fields, Francis thought upon the vision of God! When Lucy was near, he would confide, "We were all caught up in that great light which is God, and yet we did not burn. What is God like? This is something we will never be able to say! But what a pity that He is so sad! If only I could console Him!"

❉

While Lucy and Jacinta played, Francis would walk up and down in silence. They would ask him, "Francis, what are you doing?"

He would raise his arm and show them that he was saying the rosary.

"For now come to play, then we will all pray together," Lucy would say.

Francis' answer was always, "I'll pray now and afterwards, too. Don't you remember what the Blessed Mother said? I have to say many rosaries!"

Often he would leave Lucy and Jacinta alone. Later they would find him praying silently behind a low wall or a bush.

"Why don't you call us to come and pray with you?"

"Because I like to pray by myself so that I can think about God, Who is so sad because of the many sins."

Some days he simply could not be found. On one such day, when Lucy had become really worried, she found him crouched beside a stone wall, his forehead almost touching the ground. He did not answer when she called. She had to shake him until he came to himself with a start, as if waking up from sleep.

"Were you praying?" asked Lucy.

"Yes. I began with the prayers of the angel, and then I stopped to think."

"Didn't you hear Jacinta and me calling you?"

She found him crouched beside a stone wall.

"No, I didn't hear anything. I was thinking about God."

"Come, let's go to Jacinta. Poor thing! She's crying because she thinks you are lost."

It was a great sacrifice for Francis to leave those beautiful thoughts. But where would the merit be, where the consolation for God, if a sacrifice is avoided? Francis returned with Lucy. Then, when he had begun to enjoy living with the girls again, he decided to renew the sacrifice.

"I'm going back to be alone," he said, "because I want to offer this sacrifice to God."

PART II

*The sufferings of the present time
are not worthy to be compared
with the glory to come....*

St. Paul

CHAPTER 1

"YOU TWO DRINK FIRST"

The three young shepherds were inspired with great ideals: "To convert sinners;" "to console the Lord;" and "to make reparation to the Immaculate Heart of Mary."

One day, while going to the pasture, they met some poor children who lived on alms. The three shepherds had their bag of lunch, and knew for certain that these children were hungry. Jacinta had an inspiration: "Shall we give our lunch to those poor children for the conversion of sinners?"

They gave their lunch to the children and continued to do so each time they met them. For that reason they fasted practically every day. However, towards evening, they tried to satisfy their hunger by eating roots, bitter herbs, and acorns from holm-oak trees.

On one of their usual fast days, when Francis was picking acorns in a holm-oak tree, Jacinta suggested, "Let's eat the acorns of the oaks, instead!"

"But those are more bitter than these!" exclaimed Francis.

"That is why I want to eat them. We will convert more sinners!"

Lucy and Francis followed her example.

❋

One day Lucy's godmother had prepared a delicious sweet drink made of honey and water and called hydromel. She offered a glass of it to Francis. He passed it to Jacinta, saying, "You two drink first."

Then very quietly Francis left them. He did not answer their call, nor could he be found in the house. Jacinta and Lucy understood, and they, too, left the house. They were certain of finding him by Lucy's well, and they were not mistaken.

"Francis, why didn't you drink? Godmother looked all over for you!"

"Because," he answered, "as I took the glass in my hand, the thought came into my mind to make that sacrifice to console the Lord, and so I ran away."

One day while the three children were playing near the well, Mrs. Marto brought them some fresh grapes. As they were about to eat them, they seemed to hear a voice suggesting that they offer the grapes as a sacrifice. They waited until Mrs. Marto had left them. Then they took the untasted grapes to some poor friends.

Another day they had a basket of delicious figs. Just at the moment when they were about to eat the figs, Jacinta reminded them that they had not yet made any sacrifices that day. All three readily offered this as their sacrifice, each with slightly different intentions. Francis never forgot his desire of "consoling God."

✤

They say that the torment of thirst is worse than that of hunger. And yet Francis, Lucy and Jacinta passed the entire month of August without drinking a drop of water. This is a heroic sacrifice, if one recalls that they spent their days in the hot fields!

One of those days was very hot. As usual the shepherds set out early in the morning, and took the flock to a rather distant place. In order to avoid sunstroke, their parents had told them to stay in the shade and return home after sunset.

While going, they met their "little friends," the poor children to whom they had already given their lunches many times before. But this time they had more things than usual in their lunch bags. Couldn't they give away only some of it? Of course they could! But what of their generosity? Jacinta gave the example by giving away her whole lunch and Lucy and Francis joyfully did the same.

Towards noon the hot sun burned the plain with its scorching rays. Even the rocks started to break in the intense heat of that arid place. The shepherds were hungry; their tongues seemed parched with the thirst which tormented them.

How many times that day they renewed the offering of their sacrifice! "Oh, Jesus, it is for love of You, for the conversion of sinners, in reparation for the offenses against the Immaculate Heart of Mary," and *"to console You"* Francis no doubt added.

When it was past noon they couldn't resist this torment any longer. There was no water in the pasture, so they went to a small nearby village to ask for some.

They knocked at a door of a home and a good elderly lady answered. She gave them some bread and a pitcher of water. They, who had given away their lunch, gratefully accepted and ate of the bread of charity!

But when it came to the water, it was another matter. Lucy gave the pitcher to Francis, saying, "Drink!"

"I don't want to drink," he answered.

"Why not?"

"To suffer for the conversion of sinners," he promptly answered.

"You drink, Jacinta," Lucy then said.

"I want to make the sacrifice for sinners, too," she answered.

And Lucy—who also made the sacrifice for sinners—poured the water into the hollow of a rock for the sheep to drink. Then she ran joyfully to give the pitcher back to the kind lady.

But through those endless hours there was no sign of relief from the heat. Even the croaking frogs, among the unbearable chirping sounds of the grasshoppers and crickets, seemed to add to the heat of the day.

Weakened by hunger and thirst, Jacinta felt that she could endure the noise no longer.

"Go and make the frogs and crickets keep still," she said to Lucy. "My head aches so much."

"Don't you want to suffer this for sinners?" Francis asked.

Jacinta had forgotten that this, too, could be a sacrifice. But as soon as Francis reminded her, she turned to Lucy and said, "Let them sing!"

Chapter 2

"WE WOULD RATHER DIE!"

On the morning of Monday, August 13, the automobile of the mayor of the nearby town of Ourem was among the many cars speeding toward Fatima. The mayor stopped at the pastor's house, and asked him to call the three cousins. He had already questioned Lucy two days before, and had been very upset when she refused to reveal the Lady's secret.

The shepherds arrived, and answered the mayor's questions—which seemed quite friendly today. "I'd like to go to the Cova, too, today," he said. (Perhaps the Virgin had granted him a special grace to make him so friendly, Lucy thought.) "Come along," he suggested. "I'll drive you to the Cova in my car."

They had never ridden in a car before! Delighted, Lucy, Francis and Jacinta scrambled in.

But when they reached a fork in the road, the cousins realized that the car was turning toward the mayor's town, Ourem, instead of the Cova.

"No, no," they said. "The Cova is in the other direction."

"I know, I know. But first we must go to the pastor of Ourem, who wants to see you. Then we will return to the Cova. We'll still be there in time; don't worry."

✤

But he did not take them directly to the pastor, even though they asked him to do so. "First you must have lunch," declared the mayor.

They resigned themselves.

The hour for the appointment came and went. The children felt miserable. Their only consolation was in the hope that the mayor would let them go home soon.

Go home? That was not his plan at all. The mayor of Ourem had not given the children the ride for fun. He intended, not only to keep them away from the Cova, but also to learn their secret.

He questioned them for hours, but they would not tell him anything that they had been forbidden to tell.

Could it be possible that a mayor must give in to three shepherds? This was too much! "You're under arrest!" he declared, and locked them in a room with the threat, "If you want to get out, you will decide to talk; otherwise it will be all the worse for you."

They remained in that room all night long. What do you suppose they talked about during those long hours? No doubt they encouraged one another by recalling the words of the angel: "Accept with submission the sufferings which the Lord will send you." This was certainly a suffering sent by the Lord.

How many times they must have repeated the offering: "O Jesus, it is for love of You, for the conversion of sinners, and to make reparation for the offenses to the Immaculate Heart of Mary!"

The next morning they were again taken to the mayor's office, where he tried to win their confidence by offering them gold coins. Lucy spoke first, then Francis and Jacinta. All three frankly told everything which they were free to say about the apparitions, and each affirmed that they could not reveal the secret, because the Virgin had commanded them not to tell it to anyone.

❖

Again they had refused to tell the secret. This time they were cast into the public prison, among men who were thieves, bullies, and other offenders.

Jacinta cried, not in fear of the sacrifice, but because, like all little girls, she wanted to at least see her mother.

Francis gave her courage. "Patience, if we cannot see our mother! Let us offer this sacrifice for the conversion of sinners. It would be worse if the Virgin did not come back again. This would certainly displease me. But I would offer even that for the conversion of sinners."

Then he knelt down and with his hands joined in prayer, made his offering, "Jesus, it is for love of You and for the conversion of sinners."

And Jacinta added, "And also for the Holy Father and in reparation for the offenses against the Immaculate Heart of Mary." But she continued to cry. When nature rebels, a sacrifice is more precious.

The scene of the three children kneeling, with joined hands and uplifted eyes, moved some of the hardened criminals to tears. In fact, one of them advised them to reveal the secret, in order to put an end to their sufferings. But Jacinta readily answered:

"We would rather die!"

It was getting dark when they remembered that they had forgotten to say the rosary.

Jacinta made a little altar, and took off the medal which she wore around her neck. Then she asked one of the prisoners to hang it on a nail she had chosen. The three children knelt down to say the rosary.

In a short time the heavy voices of the criminals were heard in response to the silvery voices of the young shepherds.

Francis noticed that one prisoner, although on his knees, had not removed his hat.

"If you wish to pray," he told him courteously, "you should take off your hat."

The man did so immediately, and dropped it on the floor. Francis picked it up and politely set it on a bench; then he went back to his prayers.

Chapter 3

"WE'LL FRY THEM LIKE FISH!"

A few minutes later the keeper came to take Lucy, Jacinta and Francis. Were they free? Oh, no!

They were taken to the mayor's office, where he questioned them again, and again failed to obtain the secret.

"If they won't obey when treated well, then they will be forced to do so!" he shouted.

He called a guard, and loudly ordered, "Take them into the next room and prepare a pot of boiling oil. We'll fry them like fish!" The children heard the orders.

Then they were locked in the next room. After a while Jacinta was taken out.

"If you won't speak, you will be the first to be fried. Come with me."

Jacinta had stopped crying, and thought with joy that soon she would be with her Lady forever. As always, she refused to talk.

❉

In the meantime, Francis remarked to Lucy, "If they kill us, as they say they will, we will soon be in heaven. What a pleasure! To die.... It does not matter to me."

Then he thought of Jacinta. "May God keep Jacinta from being afraid," he said. "I want to say a Hail Mary for her."

He was still praying when the door opened again, and his name was called.

"She is already dead. Now it is your turn," the mayor said. But Francis remained undisturbed.

"Out with the secret!"

"The secret? No! I cannot tell it to anyone!"

"You can't tell it? We'll see! Come!" he shouted, as he roughly pulled Francis by the arm and shook him.

The results of his questioning were no different than the other ones! And Francis was shut up in another room, where he found Jacinta waiting for him! She was unharmed.

How happy they were to be together again!

Lucy, the last to be questioned, was convinced that the mayor was serious, but she was

"She is already dead. Now it is your turn!"

not afraid. She prayed to the Blessed Mother for strength, and her prayers were answered. Unable to obtain the secret from Lucy, the mayor put her in the same room with her cousins.

The next morning, after a final attempt to force the secret out, the mayor was obliged to take the three brave youngsters back to the rectory of Fatima.

How relieved their families were to have them back after two long, anxious nights!

❂

Meanwhile, what had happened at the Cova da Iria?

On August 13, fifteen thousand people had arrived there to wait for the hour of the apparition. Cars, carts, bicycles and horses were everywhere.

The hot sun blazed in the August sky—but what did this matter to the devout and curious souls whose expectations would be realized shortly?

Time dragged on. It was close to noon. Rosaries had been recited, and hymns sung, but the three young shepherds had not arrived.

What had happened? An accident? A trick? A mistake?

"WE'LL FRY THEM LIKE FISH!"

Suddenly a rumor passed through the restless crowd: the mayor of Ourem had taken the children off with him!

Imagine the indignation, anger and threats of all those people who had come for the apparition! The more excited ones wanted to go to the mayor's residence and take the children away from him by force.

Suddenly the rumble of thunder was heard. All heads turned towards the little holm-oak tree. Lightning flashed, and a white cloud appeared above the little tree!

"The Blessed Virgin!" they shouted—but they could see nothing except the cloud, as usual. After about ten minutes it disappeared. With their eyes moist with tears and their hearts filled with great joy, the people left the Cova, knowing that the Blessed Virgin had been faithful to her appointment.

Six days after the unkept appointment. the Virgin appeared to Lucy, Francis and Jacinta again. After having complained about those who had prevented the children from keeping their appointment, she told them that as a result the miracle promised for October would not be as great. As always, she added, "Pray; pray much and make sacrifices for sinners. Many souls go to hell because no one makes sacrifices for them." Then she disappeared.

Chapter 4

"THE LORD IS PLEASED...."

By this time no one doubted the sincerity of the seers. On September 13, about twenty thousand people gathered at the Cova. It was necessary to make a path through the crowd in order to let the three children pass.

Preceded by the usual signs, the Virgin appeared. She urged the children to keep on reciting the rosary for the war to end, asked them to return on the 13th of the next month, and promised that she would bring St. Joseph and the Infant Jesus with her. After a few remarks she vanished. The sun regained its noonday splendor. A mysterious shower of white flowers, as delicate as snowflakes, vanishing in mid air, had taken place during the apparition. It now ceased.

The crowd dispersed, bearing within their hearts the echo of the joy of this heavenly experience.

The seers also returned home, accompanied by their anxious and fearful parents.

"THE LORD IS PLEASED...."

❉

When going to bed that night, each of the cousins relaxed a penance which they had been offering for over fifteen days.

The inspiration for this penance had come about one day near the end of August, when they had found a rope lying on the road.

Lucy had wound it tightly around her arm. "Do you know that it hurts?" she asked joyfully. "We could tie it around our waist, and offer this sacrifice to the Lord."

Of course! This would be a most wonderful chance to suffer for sinners! They quarreled over the rope, since each had a reason for wanting it. Lucy wanted it because she had found it; Francis said that since he was going to die soon, he should have it; Jacinta wanted to close the doors of hell.... What was to be done?

A solution was soon found. With a sharp rock, they divided the rope into three pieces. They each tied a piece around their waists beneath their clothing. As the rope was coarse, it really did hurt. And in order to suffer more, Jacinta would draw the rope so tight that often she could not restrain her tears.

"Take it off," Francis would tell her, and yet he would not touch his own. That was impossible! Weren't there sinners to convert, and the Lord to console? Lucy, Jacinta and Francis wore the ropes both day and night.

But in this way they could easily ruin their health. In their generosity, the children did not realize that they should not do penance to such extremes. No one could advise them, since they never told anyone about their sacrifices and mortifications. Who could tell them to use moderation except the Virgin with whom they spoke so familiarly?

And it was the Virgin who, with loving tenderness, told them on September 13, "The Lord is pleased with your sacrifices, but He does not want you to sleep with the rope on. Wear it only during the day."

That night for the first time, they devoutly removed the ropes and hid them under their pillows. They did not want anyone else to see them.

Chapter 5

"LOOK AT THE SUN!"

October 13, 1917, dawned cold and wet. The roads were muddy from the rain which had fallen all night. Yet despite the rain, a constant stream of people kept coming to the Cova from all of Portugal.

The devout and the curious came. There were over sixty thousand persons standing beneath a forest of dripping umbrellas, anxiously awaiting the hour of the apparition.

Francis, Jacinta and Lucy had greeted that dawn with joyful hearts and thoughts turned toward the Lady.

Around noon they arrived at the Cova, well-dressed, and carrying lovely bouquets of flowers. They were nearly crushed by the pressure of the crowd about them, which caused little Jacinta to cry.

Lucy ordered the people to close their umbrellas, and, notwithstanding the fact that it was raining, the people obeyed immediately. Then Lucy started the rosary. At the sound of the noonday bells, she stopped.

"There she is! There she is!" she exclaimed. "I see her!" Lucy's face assumed a superhuman beauty and her full lips became thin and pale.

Francis and Jacinta, too, were in ecstacy.

The crowd watched them. There, next to the holm-oak tree, they saw a white cloud form about the seers, and rise up to a height of five or six yards. This happened three times.

Lucy asked, "Who are you and what do you wish?"

She received the desired answer.

"I am the Lady of the Rosary. I have come to exhort the faithful to change their way of life and stop afflicting with their sins the Lord Who is already so much offended. I have come to tell them to recite the rosary and to do penance for their sins."

The Virgin asked them to have a chapel built there in her honor. The war would end soon, she said. Then, referring to the

"LOOK AT THE SUN!"

principal reason of her apparitions, she again said, "It is necessary that sinners convert themselves and ask pardon for their sins."

Her beautiful face was veiled in sadness. Neither this sadness nor the Lady's final words were ever to be forgotten by Francis: "Let them cease to offend Our Lord, already so much offended."

These words summed up her entire message. She gazed tenderly upon the three privileged children; then, as though to salute them, she opened her hands–which reflected the sun and sent forth ribbons of light as she rose into the heavens. Lucy called out, "Look at the sun!" An immense shout rose up from the crowd.

*

The rain had stopped as though by enchantment. High, above the horizon, the sun began to appear, yet different than usual. Looking like a silvery moon, it began to spin like a large wheel of fire, sending out rays of yellow, red, green, violet, and blue light. Clouds, trees, mountains, and fields were fantastically colored by its rays and the faces of the people reflected these colors....

Twice, for an instant or more, the sun stopped, then started to turn again, raining down light and a myriad of colors....

Suddenly the crowd felt as if the sun were coming toward them. Terror, screams, professions of faith, and ardent prayers could be heard on all sides! Many fell to their knees in the mud, and humbly struck their breasts.

After ten minutes, the sun returned to its usual position, pale and without splendor. The crowd breathed a sigh of relief.

"Miracle! Miracle! Praised be Our Lady!"

The sign from heaven had come! The people's clothes, wet from the rain were now miraculously dry. People for twenty to thirty miles around had seen the miracle of the sun.

But what had the three privileged children seen?

While the Virgin had slowly risen, St. Joseph had appeared near the sun. He was holding the Infant Jesus, Who appeared as a child about a year old. The Virgin now wore a blue mantle over her white dress. An instant later, this vision vanished, to be replaced by another. Jesus Christ, in a red cloak, stood at the base of the sun. His mother stood beside Him, dressed as Our Lady of Sorrows. Jesus blessed the people; then this vision also vanished.

Chapter 6

"I CAN'T BLESS"

Even after the apparitions were over, many curious people came to Fatima to see the young shepherds and talk with them. The cousins developed a real genius for hiding themselves. One day, for instance, an automobile came down the highway with well dressed men and women in it.

"Watch and see that they are coming to look for us," Francis said. He seemed to have a special intuition for these things.

"Let's run away," Jacinta suggested.

"No, they've seen us already. Let's go ahead without any fuss, and you'll see that they won't recognize us."

The strangers stopped them.

"Do you know the three little shepherds to whom the Virgin appeared?"

"Yes we know them." Francis pretended to be calm, but he was getting worried.

"Could you tell us where they live?"

"Sure," he said quickly and happily. "Follow this road until that point, then turn to your right and then to your left. A little farther on, you'll see a house . . . " and he gave a detailed description without arousing their suspicion. The car went on.

❉

One afternoon, Mrs. Marto was worried. Francis had been missing for several hours, and could not be found. When Lucy and Jacinta entered the house she asked them to look for him.

Where would they find him? In a cave on the mountain?

"Jacinta, Lucy, I'm up here! . . ."

Why, that was Francis' voice, and it seemed to come from the ceiling! They looked up and saw him among the rafters.

"How come?" they laughingly asked him.

"Oh, there were so many people!" he explained, as he started to come down. "God willed that I be here all alone. What could I have told them? I didn't hear the Virgin speak."

❉

Urged on by the grace of God, Francis tried hard to avoid every sin and to please the Lord in all things.

One day someone asked Lucy if the Virgin had commanded her to pray for sinners.

"No," she answered.

"Jacinta, Lucy, I'm up here! . . ."

Francis, who was nearby, felt that his cousin had not told the truth. As soon as he could, he talked with her.

"Lucy," he said gently but unhappily, "You just told a lie. Whatever made you say that the Virgin did not tell us to pray for sinners?"

"If you recall," Lucy said, smiling at his anxiety, "the Virgin commanded us *to pray* for peace, that the war should end. But for the sinners, she only told us to make sacrifices."

"Oh, how true," he answered, slapping his forehead as if to say, "How absent-minded I am!"

His sense of justice was just as keen as his sense of truth. Someone had tried to convince him to let his flock browse on the edge of his godmother's field. She loved him and would not disapprove, they said. But Francis refused. He feared that this would be stealing. He only led his flock there after his godmother assured him that this would make her happy.

There was an elderly woman in Fatima who was called "Aunt Mary" by everyone. Since she was partially paralyzed, she found it hard to round up her flock of goats and sheep. They were rather wild and ran off in all directions. But when she saw Francis, Aunt Mary was relieved, for Francis would run like a squirrel to help her. He would leave right away after, without waiting to be thanked.

He was disturbed at the sight of crippled or deformed people. "I feel so sorry for them," he would say.

※

Francis could be very outspoken in the face of evil.

One day he met a woman surrounded by many people. She was a fortuneteller who pretended to bless religious articles. She made a good living from the money she charged for her "blessings."

When Francis was close by, she asked him to bless some religious articles himself. Francis kept calm, but he used this as a chance to do good.

"I can't bless," he answered, "and neither can you. Only priests can bless."

Francis' words were passed from person to person, until all the people in the village became so angry at the fortuneteller that she had to pack up her belongings and leave town for good.

Another time Francis said to Lucy, "Why are you going around with some of those girls?

Don't, because you might learn how to sin. When you come out of school, it's better for you to go to kneel at the feet of Jesus in the Blessed Sacrament, and then quickly come home alone."

And Lucy, although older than Francis, respected his advice and followed it.

"We do not know what power Francis has," people often said, "but when we are near him, we feel that we are better."

It was the reflection of his own great love for the Lord and the Virgin. This reflection shone upon others without Francis' even being aware of it. This, too, was part of his hidden mission.

CHAPTER 7

"WHAT A BEAUTIFUL LIGHT!"

When Francis went to school, his way of life changed. As he did not go to the pasture, his mother was obliged to sell the flock. Then, too, the children had to be always ready to see visitors.

Francis did not have a happy time of it at school. His thoughts were always on consoling God and saving sinners. He did not do well in his subjects, so the teacher began to make fun of him. The other boys were quick to do the same. As usual, Francis tried to stay calm and smiling, but sometimes it wasn't easy....

There was one good thing about school, though. One had to walk past the parish church. Francis would go in and kneel near the altar. It was like a corner of heaven. There, with joy in his heart, Francis felt the Divine Presence—Jesus hidden in the tabernacle. He had recently missed out on receiving his First Communion, because he had had some difficulty in stating one of the truths in the Creed, but at least he could be near God in this way....

*

The months passed. The war ended. The rattle of machine guns, the roar of cannons, the whistle of falling projectiles had finally ceased. But their echo rang in many desolate homes. How many loved ones had failed to return!

The war had taken many victims, but Spanish influenza was gathering even more. In December, 1918, about a year after the last apparition, Francis and Jacinta became ill. Would this be the fatal sickness? They multiplied their sacrifices. When Lucy visited, Jacinta would send her to Francis as a little sacrifice. Francis, in turn, would ask Lucy to do the same for Jacinta.

Although Francis grew weaker day by day, the desire for little sacrifices seemed to grow within him, to such a degree that Lucy could never find out if there really was anything he did not like. He hid his feelings about everything, in order to make more sacrifices to console the Lord.

*

"Are you suffering, Francis?" Lucy asked him one day.

"Yes, very much. But I suffer all for love of Our Lord and of the Blessed Virgin," he tried to smile, then added, "I wish I could suffer even more, Lucy, but honestly, I can't. Is the door closed tight?"

Lucy looked around to make sure. "Yes."

Weakly Francis drew something out from under the bedclothes. It was the rope which he had worn for over a year. It had three bloodstained knots in it.

"Take it," he said. "Take it away, before my mother sees it. I can't manage it any more, Lucy."

Lucy hid it and later burned it in secret. Not long thereafter she would do the same for the dying Jacinta.

✦

Francis became weaker. On some days he was unable to say the entire rosary. Although he had said many, he felt that he still had many more to say.

"Mother," he confided with regret, "I can't say the whole rosary any more. When I get half way through, my head goes around and around...."

"Pray with your heart, then, dear," his mother encouraged him. "The Virgin will be pleased just the same."

One morning Francis and Jacinta sent for Lucy. She came at once. What was it? What had happened?

The Virgin! She had come to say that she would soon take Francis with her. She also asked Jacinta if she were willing to suffer still more. Jacinta replied that she was ready to offer everything up for sinners, for the Holy Father, and for the triumph of the Immaculate Heart of Mary.

✿

On April 2, Francis' condition became alarming. His fever was very high.

"Dad," he said to his father, "I want to receive Holy Communion before I die."

"Of course you will, son," said Mr. Marto, one of the few people who had believed in the apparitions from the beginning. "I'll see about it right now." He went off to ask the pastor.

Francis sent for Lucy, who came immediately, and told her, "I have to confess myself in order to receive Holy Communion before I die. I want you to tell me if you saw me commit any sins."

After a few moments of reflection, Lucy told him, "Sometimes you disobeyed your mother when she used to tell you to stay home, and instead you came to see me."

"Yes–that's true. Thank you. Now go to Jacinta and ask her if she remembers anything else."

Jacinta remembered that once, before the apparitions, Francis had taken a few cents from his father to buy a mouth organ, and also that with some other boys he had thrown stones at boys from Boleiros.

The sick boy said, "I have already confessed those. But I will confess them again. Who knows that I didn't cause Our Lord to be sad because of these sins? But, even if I were to live, I would not commit them again. Now I am sorry." He said a quick prayer, then, turning to Lucy, he asked her to ask God to forgive him.

"I will," she answered, "but God has already forgiven you from the very fact that the Virgin said that she would soon come to take you to heaven. I'm going to Mass now, and I'll pray for you there."

"Listen," he begged, "ask Jesus to make our reverend pastor give me Holy Communion."

This was his last desire.

The pastor came. He heard Francis' confession, and promised to bring him Holy Communion the next day.

When finally the long-awaited hour arrived, Francis tried to sit up in bed to receive Holy Communion with greater reverence, but he was not permitted to do so because he was so weak. It was one more precious sacrifice to be united to many others!

That Holy Communion was one of deep joy. Francis could feel God within him just as he had when he and Jacinta drank from the angel's chalice almost three years before.

"Mother," he asked as soon as he came out of his ecstasy, "Can't I receive Our Lord again?"

Later on that day he asked his parents, his brothers and his godmother to forgive him for everything he had ever done which displeased them.

"Say a rosary for me," he begged Jacinta and Lucy. "I can't pray any more." The pain was too great.

As they prayed, he listened intently to the familiar words, "pray for us now and at the hour of our death...." He had said those words often in the many rosaries the Virgin

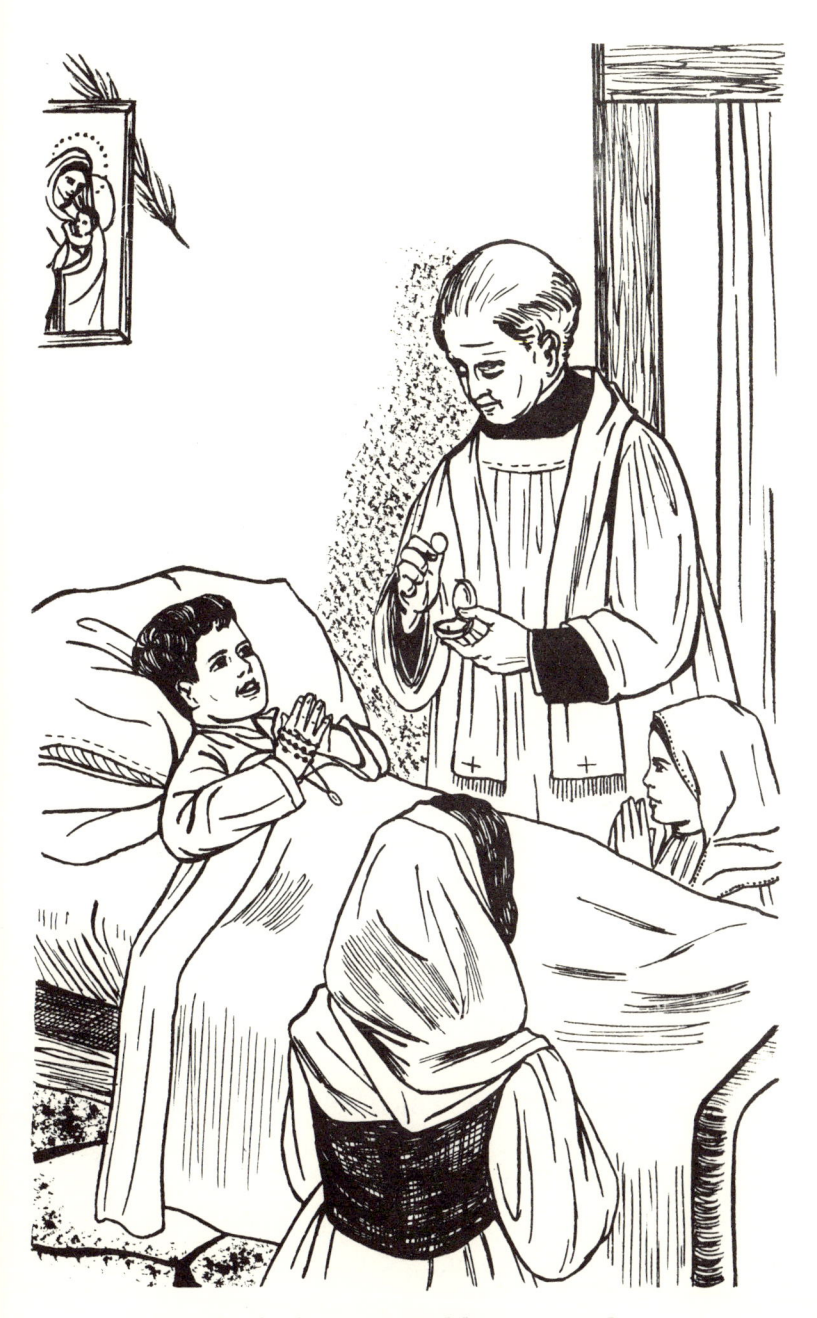

Finally the long-awaited hour arrived.

had asked him to say, but now those words had more meaning....

"Are you suffering much, Francis?" they asked him when the rosary was ended.

"Enough, but it doesn't matter; I'm suffering to console Jesus. Anyway, soon I'll go to heaven."

He looked at Jacinta. He'd be seeing her soon.

He looked at Lucy. What would he ever do without her in heaven? He did not hesitate to say, "I'm going to miss you. Oh, if only the Virgin would call you to heaven soon, too!"

❊

Lucy left Francis late that night.

"Goodbye, Francis! If you go to paradise tonight, don't forget me up there!"

"I'll never forget you; be sure of that!"

Taking her hand, he pressed it to him tightly. Tears began to fill his eyes.

"Is there something else you want to say?" Lucy asked.

"No." Francis' voice died in his throat.

The scene was becoming so tense that Mrs. Marto begged the girls to leave the room.

"Goodbye, then, Francis, till we meet in heaven," said Lucy.

"I'll be seeing you, up there!" he answered.

Jacinta lingered a few minutes longer! "Bring my greetings to Our Lord and the Blessed Mother," she said. "Tell them that I will suffer as much as they want for the conversion of sinners, and to make reparation to the Immaculate Heart."

Francis smiled.

Jacinta left the room, and in a few minutes her brother was fast asleep, while his mother watched him anxiously.

※

Strong sunlight was pouring in the window on that morning of April 4, 1919. Francis called out, "Mother!"

"Are you in pain, Francis?"

He did not answer. He was smiling. "Look, Mother—there near the door! What a beautiful light!"

He smiled sweetly, and breathed his last breath.

On the following day four boys in white suits carried the little coffin to the cemetery. The pastor and several men followed. Behind them walked Lucy and all the Marto family except Jacinta, who was too sick to come. All of them were weeping.

Francis was buried in a simple grave with no headstone, marked only by the plain cross which Lucy placed beside it. Probably Lucy reflected on how right the plain grave was for Francis. It was as hidden as his mission had been. He wouldn't have wanted it any other way.

Daughters of St. Paul

IN MASSACHUSETTS
  50 St. Paul's Ave. Jamaica Plain, Boston, MA 02130;
   617-522-8911; 617-522-0875;
  172 Tremont Street, Boston, MA 02111; **617-426-5464;**
   617-426-4230
IN NEW YORK
  78 Fort Place, Staten Island, NY 10301; **212-447-5071**
  59 East 43rd Street, New York, NY 10017; **212-986-7580**
  7 State Street, New York, NY 10004; **212-447-5071**
  625 East 187th Street, Bronx, NY 10458; **212-584-0440**
  525 Main Street, Buffalo, NY 14203; **716-847-6044**
IN NEW JERSEY
  Hudson Mall — Route 440 and Communipaw Ave.,
   Jersey City, NJ 07304; **201-433-7740**
IN CONNECTICUT
  202 Fairfield Ave., Bridgeport, CT 06604; **203-335-9913**
IN OHIO
  2105 Ontario St. (at Prospect Ave.), Cleveland, OH 44115; **216-621-9427**
  25 E. Eighth Street, Cincinnati, OH 45202; **513-721-4838**
IN PENNSYLVANIA
  1719 Chestnut Street, Philadelphia, PA 19103; **215-568-2638**
IN FLORIDA
  2700 Biscayne Blvd., Miami, FL 33137; **305-573-1618**
IN LOUISIANA
  4403 Veterans Memorial Blvd., Metairie, LA 70002; **504-887-7631;**
   504-887-0113
  1800 South Acadian Thruway, P.O. Box 2028, Baton Rouge, LA 70821
   504-343-4057; 504-343-3814
IN MISSOURI
  1001 Pine Street (at North 10th), St. Louis, MO 63101; **314-621-0346;**
   314-231-1034
IN ILLINOIS
  172 North Michigan Ave., Chicago, IL 60601; **312-346-4228**
IN TEXAS
  114 Main Plaza, San Antonio, TX 78205; **512-224-8101**
IN CALIFORNIA
  1570 Fifth Avenue, San Diego, CA 92101; **714-232-1442**
  46 Geary Street, San Francisco, CA 94108; **415-781-5180**
IN HAWAII
  1143 Bishop Street, Honolulu, HI 96813; **808-521-2731**
IN ALASKA
  750 West 5th Avenue, Anchorage AK 99501; **907-272-8183**
IN CANADA
  3022 Dufferin Street, Toronto 395, Ontario, Canada
IN ENGLAND
  128, Notting Hill Gate, London W11 3QG, England
  133 Corporation Street, Birmingham B4 6PH, England
  5A-7 Royal Exchange Square, Glasgow G1 3AH, England
  82 Bold Street, Liverpool L1 4HR, England
IN AUSTRALIA
  58 Abbotsford Rd., Homebush, N.S.W., Sydney 2140, Australia

PROPERTY OF
St. Benedict's School Library
2306 Bedford St.
Johnstown, Pa. 15904

DATE DUE

APR 21 1988